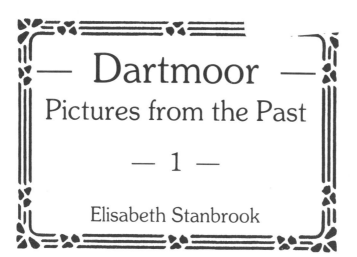

— Dartmoor —
Pictures from the Past

— 1 —

Elisabeth Stanbrook

QUAY
PUBLICATIONS
(BRIXHAM)

ISBN 1 870083 00 8

Published by Quay Publications (Brixham),
P.O. Box 16, Brixham, Devon TQ5 8LW

Typeset by AJL Typesetting, Paignton, Devon.
Telephone: (0803) 526103

Printed in Great Britain
by The Devonshire Press Ltd.
Torquay, Devon

Front Cover:
Horns & Dendles
(G. H. Jenkins Jr.)
Raphael Tuck & Sons

Acknowledgements

The author would like to thank the following people for their kind assistance in the compiling of
this book: Mr Elliot, Buckland; Mrs Hunt, Manaton; Manor House Hotel, North Bovey; Mr S. J.
Moore, Gidleigh; Mr G. Morgan, Manaton; Mrs Webb, Postbridge; Mr Dick Wills, Ilsington
and the West Country Studies Library, Exeter.

Plate Acknowledgements

Plates 17, 21, 22, 24, 26, 31, 35, 51, 54, 56, 57 and 58 are reproduced by kind permission of the
Devon Library Services, Exeter.

Plates 13 and 53 kindly lent by Mary Stanbrook.

Plates 3, 23, 32, 34, 38, 40 and 59 kindly lent by Richard Stanbrook.

List of Plates

Plate 1. *Meavy* Unknown   6

Plate 2. *Sheepstor* W. R. Gay   8

Plate 3. *Hellington, Sheepstor* Chapman & Son   8

Plate 4. *Burrator Reservoir* Chapman & Son   10

Plate 5. *Burrator Reservoir, with Cross Gate Cross in foreground.* Chapman & Son   10

Plate 6. *Yelverton* W. R. Gay   12

Plate 7. *Merrivale and the Staple Tors* Chapman & Son   12

Plate 8. *Tavistock, West Street* F. Frith & Co.   14

Plate 9. *Tavistock, the River Tavy* Chapman & Son   14

Plate 10. *The Mill at Peter Tavy* Chapman & Son   16

Plate 11. *Mary Tavy village and church* F. Frith & Co.   16

Plate 12. *Lydford Mill* F. Frith & Co.   18

Plate 13. *A cottage at Lydford* Chapman & Son   18

Plate 14. *The military at Okehampton* Lugg & Sons   20

Plate 15. *R.A. Practice Camp at Okehampton* Chapman & Son   20

Plate 16. *Taw Marsh near Okehampton* Unknown   22

Plate 17. *Cranmere Pool* Unknown   22

Plate 18. *West Okement near Meldon Viaduct* Chapman & Son   24

Plate 19. *Dartmoor Guide in front of Yes Tor & West Mill Tor* Chapman & Son   24

Plate 20. *South Tawton* Chapman & Son   26

Plate 21. *The church at Belstone* Unknown   26

Plate 22. *Teignhead clapper bridge* Unknown   28

Plate 23. *Fernworthy clapper bridge* Valentine & Son   28

Plate 24. *Throwleigh* Chapman & Son   30

Plate 25. *Berrydown, Gidleigh* Chapman & Son   30

Plate 26. *Lower Street, Chagford* Chapman & Son   32

Plate 27. *The Market Square, Chagford* Valentine & Son   32

Plate 28. *Fingle Bridge Tea Shelter* Chapman & Son   34

Plate 29. *Drewsteignton* Chapman & Son   36

Plate 30. *Jay's Grave, near Manaton* Chapman & Son   38

Plate 31. *Foxworthy Mill, near Lustleigh* Unknown   38

Plate 32. *Manor House, North Bovey* Chapman & Son   40

Plate 33. *Hall House, Lustleigh* Unknown   40

Plate 34. *Bellever Tor and the Cherrybrook* Unknown   42

Plate 35. *Pound Street, Moretonhampstead* Chapman & Son   42

Plate 36. *Warren House Inn, near Postbridge* Unknown   44

Plate 37. *Inside the Warren House Inn* Charles Worcester & Co.   44

Plate 38. *Temperance Hotel, Postbridge* Chapman & Son   46

Plate 39. *Old and New Bridges, Ockery* Kingsway Seines   46
Plate 40. *Princetown and the Duchy Hotel* Chapman & Son   48
Plate 41. *Prison officers at Princetown* F. Frith & Co.   48
Plate 42. *Two Bridges Hotel* Unknown   50
Plate 43. *Two Bridges Hotel* Unknown   50
Plate 44. *River Dart in flood at Dartmeet, 1938* Chapman & Son   52
Plate 45. *River Dart in flood at Dartmeet, 1938* Chapman & Son   52
Plate 46. *Widecombe-in-the-Moor* Unknown   54
Plate 47. *Uncle Tom Cobleigh and all.* E. Scott   54
Plate 48. *Beatrice Chase* Chapman & Son   56
Plate 49. *Venton Cottage* Chapman & Son   58
Plate 50. *Interior of Venton Chapel* Chapman & Son   58
Plate 51. *Holne Park, Ashburton* Chapman & Son   60
Plate 52. *Lower Lodge, Buckland* Chapman & Son   60
Plate 53. *Buckfast Abbey before restoration* W. R. Gay   62
Plate 54. *Rebuilding of Buckfast Abbey* Unknown   62
Plate 55. *Church Steps, Buckfastleigh* Chapman & Son   64
Plate 56. *South Brent, Station Road and Square* Unknown   66
Plate 57. *Moorlands Hotel, Haytor* Unknown   66
Plate 58. *Ilsington* Chapman & Son   68
Plate 59. *Ilsington* Unknown   68
Plate 60. *Pinchaford, near Ilsington* Chapman & Son   70

Introduction

One item that is increasingly sought after by collectors is the postcard. It is the older photographic postcards that are of particular interest as they provide an invaluable insight into times long since gone. They are an all important visual record of changes that have occurred during the last century, to buildings, the countryside, methods of transport and even styles of clothing. They also show scenes that no longer exist; scenes of which rising generations would otherwise only be able to read about.

Apart from the professional photographer and the enthusiastic amateur, the ownership of photographic material was by no means as widespread as it is today. Hence there is not the abundance of pictorial information dating from the turn of the century that future historians will enjoy dating from the mid century onwards.

Perhaps the most notable postcard photographer, certainly for the Dartmoor and South Devon area, was the firm Chapman & Son of Dawlish who published postcards for four generations. The distinctive backward sloping writing on each card was undertaken by Lillian Chapman, granddaughter of the firm's founder, William James Chapman. William R. Gay of South Brent also produced high quality photographs and his production of postcards was most prolific during 1911 to 1924. Frith, Judges and Tuck & Sons are also well known names in the Devon postcard industry, who all supplied the public with views either of their locality or of their holiday resort.

When first starting out as a keen collector of Dartmoor postcards and photographs, it very quickly became apparent that these photographers provided a wealth of social history through the lens. This book is therefore largely intended for the reader who enjoys a visual glimpse into a bygone age.

Plate 1. *Meavy* Unknown

1. Meavy

The parish of Meavy, covering about six square miles, lies on the south-west fringes of Dartmoor. The Domesday Survey records the name as Metwi, when it passed to Judael of Totnes. Over the centuries the name has changed and a document of 1589 shows the name as Meavie, not dissimilar from today's spelling.

The Church of St. Peter was consecrated in 1122, although the structure we see today is largely fifteenth century. Remains of an earlier building are evident, such as the mouldings on the chancel arch, believed to be Norman.

The village cross by the five little girls, is a restoration. During the late nineteenth century, the only signs that a cross once stood here were the base and pedestal. At some later date, a highly inappropriate granite post was inserted into this base. Writing at the time, Robert Burnard commented that it would be "a credit to the parish if a new shaft were procured on the pattern of that at Marchant's Cross, and inserted in the old base". This proved to be unnecessary because in 1882, Rev. W.A.G. Gray found the original octagonal shaft which was serving as a gatepost nearby. Various other cross fragments came to light, and with a new head and arms, restoration was completed in 1895. Today it still stands proud at eleven feet high.

The oak tree to the left of the cross is very ancient but it has so far not been accurately dated. Hence the various traditions arising as to when it was planted. One belief is that it is the same age as the church while another claims it was planted during the reign of King John, between 1199 and 1216. Similar trees were then planted at Tamerton and Buckland Monachorum. Whatever its age, it is obviously of great antiquity. It is virtually hollow inside, and for a considerable number of years has had to be supported by sturdy posts.

The building on the left is the Royal Oak Inn, formerly the Church House which was built during the fifteenth century. There is an interesting entry in the Parish Minutes in 1887: "Trouble about the Royal Oak Inn: the Tenant became indebted to the suppliers of Liquors — Messrs Vosper. 'At present the House is badly supplied with drinks, often being without Ale for 2 or 3 days together and all owing to the management of the House'. It was agreed that a new landlord be found".

The wording on one of the carts is "Maker of Hovis" and it is likely that a delivery is being made to the inn.

Plate 2. *Sheepstor* W. R. Gay

Plate 3. *Hellington, Sheepstor* Chapman & Son

2 & 3. Sheepstor

The village of Sheepstor lies near the banks of the River Meavy, overshadowed by the massive granite tor from which it takes its name. Apart from the magnificent views seen from this tor, it is well known for the "Pixies Cave", a large chamber formed between large slabs of granite. It is here that a member of the Elford family, who were Lords of Longstone Manor and fervent Royalists, sought refuge during the turmoil of the Civil War. Villagers entrusted with this information endeavoured to keep him provided with food for the duration of his confinement. There is no evidence to support this tradition, only stories passed down through the generations telling how paintings were found on the walls of the cave, which were executed by Elford to pass the time.

Longstone remained a manor until John Elford's death in September, 1748, when it became used as a farmhouse. The family name lived on in the area but they were seen as poor relations.

It is not known for certain to whom the church at Sheepstor was dedicated, but it is thought to be St Leonard. It has an unusual stone above the porch, carved to form a skull and crossbones with wheat protruding from the eye sockets. It is likely that it once belonged to a tomb. The church is mainly sixteenth century, built of granite with the windows carved from Roborough stone. Buried in the churchyard is Sir James Brooke of Sarawak and his nephew. Sir James's tomb is made from red granite brought from Aberdeen. Also buried here are Amos Shillibeer, the Devonport Leat foreman, and his brother William who lived at Higher Lowery.

The Holy Well of St Leonard can be found in the churchyard wall in Tor Lane, opposite Pitts Cottage. Its granite canopy is from a window in the church. The well used to be sited in a field near the church, but in the 1890s, the rector moved the water supply to its present site for the convenience of the villagers.

The fifteenth century Priest's House used to be a vicarage. It then became an alehouse offering refreshment and hospitality to traders, usually jobbers. Sheepstor was situated on the Jobber's Path, the route running from Buckfastleigh to Tavistock. These men were involved in the wool trade, delivering fleece, yarn and cloth. Two buildings in the same field as the House were used for the pack horses. The Priest's House eventually became the Parish Room. Other industries in the area were farming and tin mining.

It is evident that bull baiting was once a popular sport here. The vicarage field used for such occasions still has the bull ring. This venue was also used for other sports such as cock fighting and wrestling.

At the turn of the nineteenth century, Sheepstor boasted a small inn —Park Cottage Inn — owned by Mr Nelder. Trade was brisk due to a large local workforce of farmers, miners and men working on Burrator Reservoir and Sheepstor Dam. However, the decline of these industries saw the close of this hostelry. It was demolished before World War Two.

The bottom photograph shows Hellington, situated near to the church. It used to provide a tea room, but not any longer.

Plate 4. *Burrator Reservoir* Chapman & Son

Plate 5. *Burrator Reservoir, with Cross Gate Cross in foreground.*
Chapman & Son

4 & 5. Burrator Reservoir

From 1591 until 1898, the port of Plymouth relied upon Drake's Leat to supply its water requirements. As the port grew in size, this leat became inadequate for the town's needs.

In January 1881, a heavy snowstorm blocked the leat cutting off Plymouth's water supply for weeks resulting in terrible hardships, especially amongst the poorer classes. Manufacturers needing water were compelled to shut down the factories and the population became wholly dependent upon wells. The military, aided by civilians, were eventually able to clear the leat at a cost of £700. Ten years later in 1891, another appalling winter gripped the country. Again, Plymouth's water supply was cut off and it was cleared by the military at a cost of £2,000.

To supply Plymouth with an alternative water supply was now an urgent matter. The first site favoured by Plymouth Corporation was the Head Weir of the leat, owned by Sir Massey Lopes who refused to sell it. Instead he tried to sell them his Hartor site for £5,000. There was so much public opposition to both sites that eventually they were abandoned in favour of Burrator Gorge, proposed by Edward Sandeman, which would submerge several houses including Longstone Manor, seat of the Elford family.

The first sod was cut at the Fyshing Feaste on 9th August, 1893, and the pipe line was completed in 1894. The actual reservoir was finished in September, 1898 and had taken over 400 men continuously employed for five years to construct it. There had been only two deaths on the site. A quarter of the men were housed in corrugated iron dwellings erected at Burrator by the Corporation, and the rest found lodgings in nearby villages.

To commemorate the opening of Burrator Reservoir, schoolchildren were presented with special medals inscribed on one side with the words "Commenced 9th Aug 1893; area 116 acres; capacity 651,000,000 gallons" and an engraving of the dam. On the other side "Plymouth 21st Sept — 1898. The Burrator Reservoir, constructed to avert the danger and hardship to which the town was formerly liable, was this day completed; this medal was struck to commemorate the event, and is the gift of J.T. Bond, Mayor 1891-1896-1898."

In 1926, Burrator Dam was heightened and a suspension bridge seen here, acted as a temporary measure to carry the Sheepstor road across the valley.

A secondary dam at Sheepstor was built to prevent the overflow of the reservoir at a point where the land dips a little.

Plate 6. *Yelverton* W. R. Gay

Plate 7. *Merrivale and the Staple Tors* Chapman & Son

6. Yelverton

Yelverton is usually thought of as being a Victorian town. However, its history can be traced back to at least 1291 when documentation records it as Elleford and was probably no more than a farmstead. Then in the fifteenth century, the Elford family moved to the vicinity and lived in a house known as "Elford Town".

It remained a small village until the opening of the railway station in 1885. This led to expansion with the opening of shops and hotels, making it a popular holiday resort. World War Two saw the development of the Harrowbeer Aerodrome, which was mainly an emergency airfield. The upper storeys of the shops had to be removed as they lay within the flight path. Harrowbeer closed in 1945.

This photograph shows Yelverton Rock near the aerodrome site. This was a popular place for picnics and although the aerodrome and railway have long since gone, remains an attraction.

7. Merrivale and the Staple Tors

Merrivale has changed very little over the years. Taken around 1910, this photograph shows the Tor Granite Quarry which belonged to William Duke. Due to the demand for granite, he opened this quarry in 1876 and it was managed for a time by William Bolt. It continued the sett-making craft that had been in operation in the nearby Staple Tor Quarry during the early 1870s. These setts were used for street paving. Corbels, pillars and gravestones were also produced.

The row of white houses was erected for the use of the quarry workers, but they have now been demolished. Today the quarry is owned by the Dartmoor Granite Company.

The bridge spans the River Walkham which marks the boundary between Walkhampton Common and Whitchurch parish.

The Little, Middle and Great Staple Tors are impressive and the latter boasts good examples of rock basins.

Plate 8. *Tavistock, West Street* F. Frith & Co.

Plate 9. *Tavistock, the River Tavy* Chapman & Son

8 & 9. Tavistock

This top view is of West Street, which leads down to the Bedford Square. Lord John Russell was granted the town of Tavistock after the Dissolution and became the Duke of Bedford. In the nineteenth century, one of his descendants, Francis, had the slums and narrow streets replaced with new buildings including those in Bedford Square. A statue was erected in this square in 1848 to commemorate the Duke of Bedford's enhancement of this town.

The church in the picture is that of St Eustachius which is mentioned as far back as 1265. There are only two other churches in England dedicated to this saint, one in Dorset and the other in Sussex. Eustachius was a Roman officer who turned to christianity after experiencing a holy vision. The church has undergone some alterations since the thirteenth century. Behind the church rises Cock's Tor.

West Street had two schools in the 1890s. One was run by Mr R.M. Thornton and called "Tavistock Middle Class School for Day Boys and Boarders" and the other was a "School of Art" run by Mr W. Middleton.

There was also a small cottage hospital here, but in the late 1890s it was replaced by a larger one in Launceston Road.

At the turn of the century road surfaces were very rough, usually made of gravel or grit with a tendency to be dusty or muddy, depending upon the weather. The rough surface can be seen here, especially on the left-hand side of the picture.

Horses and carts were the usual form of transport and the cart in the foreground bears the words "Estimates Free" and presumably belonged to a local business.

In the lower photograph can be seen some of the remains of Tavistock Abbey on the banks of the River Tavy. The Abbey was founded in 975 by Ordulf and was completed in 981. Misfortune struck in 997 when the invading Danes burnt it down. However, it was rebuilt and continued to flourish until the reign of Henry VIII, who authorised the dissolution of the monasteries in 1539.

Today only a few ruins remain and these include the fifteenth century Betsy Grimbal's Tower and the Higher Abbey Gate. This photograph shows the Still House which was situated near the Abbots' Herb Garden and is thought to have been used for preparing and distilling the herbs for use in the Abbey Infirmary. The tower fell into disrepair last century but was renovated in 1884.

The riverside walk on the opposite bank of the Tavy is known as St John's Avenue.

Plate 10. *The Mill at Peter Tavy* Chapman & Son

Plate 11. *Mary Tavy village and church* F. Frith & Co.

10. The Mill at Peter Tavy

The village of Peter Tavy is situated about three miles north of Tavistock amidst some impressive scenery. This old mill, known as the Higher Mill, is now no longer in use. It is tucked away in a particularly lovely part of the village and can be admired while following the route to Peter Tavy Combe. It is a building that has been the subject of many paintings and sketches, some of which, according to Mrs Elizabeth Bray, were exhibited in the Water-colour Exhibitions at Somerset House. The public were apparently always eager to buy.

Following the Colly Brook upstream, a clam or wooden bridge can be crossed and the path takes one up to Great Combe Tors from where there are splendid panoramic views of the surrounding countryside below. The churches of both Peter Tavy and the sister village of Mary Tavy are clearly visible, together with a distant view of Brentor Church.

11. Mary Tavy

At the time of the Domesday Survey, the Manor of Mary Tavy belonged to Judael of Totnes. The actual village is an ancient settlement lying beside the Cholwell Brook which joins the River Tavy below Longtimber Tor, half a mile away. Many of the houses seen today were built during the last century to accommodate the miners and quarrymen who were actively employed in the area.

The mines closely connected with the village were those of Wheals Betsy, Friendship and Jewell, and their main yields were tin, copper, silver and arsenic. Wheal Friendship was the richest copper mine and workings started here before 1796, continuing until 1925. It had the longest history of working than any other mine in Devon and Cornwall. Records suggest that these three mines attracted a large workforce from East Cornwall as well as Mary Tavy and the surrounding area.

On part of the site occupied by the Wheal Friendship mine now stands the hydro-electric power station which supplies current to the National Grid, although it can be used locally if necessary.

The church is dedicated to St Mary and is mostly fifteenth and sixteenth century. It was restored in 1878-9. The granite cross in the churchyard is the village cross. In 1880, the churchyard was extended to include the cross and village green upon which it stood.

During the 1890s, Mary Tavy became the home of William Crossing and his wife Emma. They are both buried in the churchyard.

Plate 12. *Lydford Mill* F. Frith & Co.

Plate 13. *A cottage at Lydford* Chapman & Son

18

12 & 13. Lydford

Lydford's history can be traced back to at least the Saxon age. During the ninth century, King Alfred decided that four defensive towns were necessary to defend against impending invasion from the Danes. Lydford was chosen as one of the four and it soon became a town of some importance. The other three were Totnes, Exeter and Barnstaple.

Lydford was an administrative centre during the tenth and eleventh centuries and even produced coins from its own mint which was situated in Silver Street.

In 997, the defences of Lydford were tested when the Danes were rampaging through the area. Having burnt Tavistock Abbey, they moved northwards to Lydford, but were unsuccessful in destroying the town. It is thought possible that they burnt the original wooden church but there is no firm evidence to support this.

Lydford maintained her importance over the next few centuries as her administrative duties covered the whole of the Forest of Dartmoor. The imposing castle, built in 1195, was used as a prison for those transgressing both the Forest laws and the Stannary laws.

The church is dedicated to St Petrock which suggests Lydford was occupied by the Celts. The present building is thirteenth century with fifteenth and nineteenth century additions. To the west of the churchyard, a Norman defensive bank can be seen.

The importance of Lydford gradually declined, partly due to the development of neighbouring towns such as Tavistock and Okehampton, both of which had regular markets.

The decline of Lydford was to such an extent that Baring-Gould was prompted to write that during the 1800s, "The people were a law to themselves, and had the credit of being inveterate poachers. The houses, thatched, built of moor-stones, not set in mortar, were in a ruinous condition. The aspect of the place was that of an Irish village." The church did not escape criticism as it was "fast lapsing to ruin, and was girt in by walls long ago reduced to heaps".

Happily, Lydford was restored and became the attractive well kept village we see today. Some of the thatched cottages have had tile roof replacements and the old corn mill no longer functions, but it is now a favourite place for visitors.

Plate 14. *The military at Okehampton* Lugg & Sons

Plate 15. *R.A. Practice Camp at Okehampton* Chapman & Son

20

14 & 15. Okehampton Camp

In 1872, a local paper carried the report that Dartmoor had been selected for the following year's Autumn Manoeuvres. Although Cannock Chase, between Birmingham and Lichfield, had been favoured by the military authorities for some considerable time, Dartmoor was finally chosen as being nearer to the probable scene of an invasion.

A total of 12,000 men and 2,100 horses arrived on Dartmoor in 1873 and set up their camps at Yennadon and Ringmoor Down. So successful were these camps that the War Office selected a more permanent site near Okehampton which was established in August, 1875, under the command of Lt. Col. Todd Browne, RHA. The army utilized a substantial acreage between the East Okement and Taw rivers for their firing practices.

From 1877 these camps were held annually, lasting for a duration of six weeks at first, but then extending to a longer period of time.

The War Department decided that as Dartmoor had proved such an ideal location for military manoeuvres, they would apply to the Duchy of Cornwall for a licence to use the northern quarter of the moor as an artillery range, designating the area as a danger zone. This licence was granted and the military were able to lease an area of fifteen square miles. The commoners were awarded compensation for the consequential disturbance of their rights.

Five years later, in 1900, there was further agitation from the War Department to acquire more land for military use. Lord Ebrington and the Chairman of the Dartmoor Committee of the Devon County Council were anxious that the government should obtain Dartmoor as a training ground for troops as the Okehampton site was proving so successful for artillery training. But there was a fear that there might be difficulty in obtaining the land due to public opposition.

Difficulty or not, the War Office managed to acquire Willsworthy manor, including the notable Tavy Cleave, and a year later, in 1901, the Military Manoeuvres Bill was introduced. This proposed that the whole of the Dartmoor area should be used for a period of 20 days for artillery practice, giving only two weeks' notice and allowing no access to the area. So strong was the opposition to this Bill that it was eventually dropped.

The army presence on the moor was by now firmly established. The first gun practice at night took place in July, 1905 at Okehampton Camp. In 1906-7 nearly seven miles of tracks were laid and as mechanisation became more widespread, many of these tracks were made into tarmac roads. Opposition to the military presence had been great but it was here to stay, with increased activity during the two world wars.

Dartmoor had been used as a training area long before 1873. During the Napoleonic and Crimean Wars, and in the 1860s, there were several military exercises here. Voluntary camps were also held in areas such as Haytor Down. But it was the 1873 Autumn Manoeuvres that saw the beginnings of a permanent military presence on one of England's most beautiful areas.

Plate 16. *Taw Marsh near Okehampton* Unknown

Plate 17. *Cranmere Pool* Unknown

16. Taw Marsh

This photograph was taken south of Belstone on the banks of the River Taw which was a popular picnic spot. The two tors in the background are those of Steeperton on the left and Oke on the right. The river rises half a mile from Cranmere Pool and, as Crossing comments, "From Belstone there is no better place for reaching Cranmere than to trace the Taw to its source". It flows through some fine scenery, passing by the ruins of Knack Mine and into Steeperton Gorge, west of the tor. At the tor's north foot, the river joins the Steeperton Brook which flows on the tor's eastern side.

In 1957 Taw Marsh was the site for trial boreholes, ordered by the North Devon Water Board. They were testing for an underground lake to cope with increasing demands for water. The tests proved positive and a Bill was introduced to install wells and pumping stations. Unfortunately, the water was discovered to be radio-active and an aeration plant had to be erected north of Taw Marsh to extract the radon gas.

17. Cranmere Pool

Situated on the northern moor this spot is one of Dartmoor's most famous landmarks and despite its name, the actual water here is minimal. It is interesting to look at the measurements taken by William Crossing in 1881. He found it to be one hundred and ninety two feet in circumference, with its deepest part at the eastern end where the bank was ten feet high.

Here we can see the site of the letterbox established by James Perrott in 1854, which is now marked by a modern structure erected in 1937. Letterboxing is a custom which has remained with us and which has spread to all parts of the moor.

Cranmere Pool is reputed to be haunted by the spirit of Benjamin Gayer, a wealthy merchant and former mayor of Okehampton. A misdemeanor on his part resulted in his spirit being condemned to empty the water from the pool with a sieve. Sometimes his sobbing can be heard as he goes about this task.

Although once difficult to reach, the military roads from Okehampton have made access easy and one can now get to within approximately one mile of Cranmere Pool.

Plate 18. *West Okement near Meldon Viaduct* Chapman & Son

Plate 19. *Dartmoor Guide in front of Yes Tor & West Mill Tor*
    Chapman & Son

24

18. Meldon

This shows the site of Meldon Reservoir near Okehampton, long before work began on its construction in 1970. In 1962, the North Devon Water Authority announced that a new reservoir was necessary to cope with the demand from its southern division. This area was chosen as being the most suitable, but fierce opposition from various bodies resulted in a public enquiry in March, 1965. This took sixteen months, after which Meldon was still favoured. The Houses of Parliament were petitioned and there was a hearing in 1967. Costs for an alternative site at Gorhuish proved to be far more expensive so Meldon was the final choice.

The dam was built of concrete and the surface area of the reservoir is 57 acres, with a capacity of 680 million gallons. Meldon Reservoir was finally opened on 22nd September, 1972, by Sir Peter Mills, MP.

The West Okement river, on flowing out of the reservoir, travels through Meldon Quarry and Okehampton Park to below the castle where it joins the East Okement river to form the River Okement. This in turn eventually joins the River Torridge.

19. Yes Tor and West Mill Tor

These imposing granite masses of Yes Tor and West Mill Tor are situated on northern Dartmoor and can be easily reached from Okehampton and the nearby military camp. These are two of the tors that form a range from Halstock Down in the north-east to the West Okement in the south-west. The other tors are Row Tor and High Willies.

Both tors are situated within the Army ranges and Yes Tor has a military flag pole and an OS Triangulation Point. Standing at a height of 2030 feet, it was once thought to be the highest of Dartmoor's tors but in fact, this honour belongs to High Willies. Yes Tor also has nearby prehistoric remains made evident by a nearby cairn. Flint flakes have also been found in the vicinity. The name Yes Tor is thought to have evolved from the word "Ernestorre", meaning Eagle's Tor. However, such magnificent birds are not to be found here today.

Baring-Gould claims that the granite of West Mill Tor is of a peculiar nature. Apparently, the feldspar is so pure that some people have attempted to make soda-water bottles from it by "fusing without the adjunct of other materials".

In the foreground of the photograph is the Redaven Brook and standing beside it is one of the Dartmoor guides.

Plate 20. *South Tawton* Chapman & Son

Plate 21. *The church at Belstone* Unknown

20. South Tawton

This village on the northern edge of Dartmoor, takes its name from one of the largest parishes in Devon, covering an area of 11,000 acres. Before the Norman Conquest, South Tawton was an ancient demesne which formed part of the dowry of Gytha, mother of King Harold.

It is referred to in the Domesday Survey as Tauetona, and was one of the manors in the Hundred of Wonford. In 1219, Henry III gave to Roger de Tony the manor of South Tawton, which remained in the Tony Family until the fourteenth century when it passed into the possession of the Earls of Warwick.

The church, dedicated to St Andrew, is largely fourteenth century although the tower was built a century later. It is likely a church stood on the site before the present building was constructed. The old thatched granite Church House dates from the fourteenth century and was used for accommodating the clergy, and also for brewing ale and baking bread for village functions.

In the centre of the village is the Cross Tree. The elm which once stood inside the granite surround has been replaced by an oak. It is thought that it may have served as a boundary of Town Barton Farm. Other claims are that a cross once stood here, or that it marks the crossroads.

There are good examples of typical thatched Devon cottages to be found in South Tawton.

21. The Church at Belstone

Belstone, one of Dartmoor's northern border villages, is situated about two and half miles south-east of Okehampton.

The granite church is dedicated to St Mary and the first rector recorded on the Roll was in 1260. Throughout the centuries the church seems to have been kept in good condition, according to the 1745 Archidiaconal Visitation Report, which says, "The furniture of the church and chancel is in every respect agreable to ye Canon". However, a rapid decay in its condition appears to have taken place because in the 1871 Report, it is stated that, "Unless the church is restored, it must fall ... the flooring is very damp ... the books are very bad ... the ceiling falling in". Luckily, restoration took place in 1881 at a cost of £800, but much of the old interior was lost. It was a restoration that did not receive the approval of all, but without it, more permanent damage would have been inevitable.

Plate 22. *Teignhead clapper bridge* Unknown

Plate 23. *Fernworthy clapper bridge* Valentine & Son

28

22. Teignhead Clapper Bridge

This bridge spans the North Teign river not far from Teignhead Farm, and has a length of about twenty seven feet. It is not the best example of a clapper bridge on Dartmoor but it nevertheless serves as useful a purpose as the more impressive ones. It was built during the second half of the eighteenth century by a Mr Rogers who erected the nearby Teignhead Farm and enclosed fourteen hundred acres of the surrounding moor.

This farm passed through the hands of several farmers before its final owner vacated the premises in 1940. They included Mr Dodd, Mr Endacott, Mr Gamlin, Mr Lamb of Prince Hall and Mr Hamlyn. The last owner was George Hutchins.

James Perrott can be seen standing to the left of the bridge. A well-known and respected guide, he was often asked to take photographers to remote places.

23. Fernworthy

The ancient clapper bridge seen here, which spanned the South Teign river, is now submerged under Fernworthy Reservoir together with an early twentieth century arched bridge.

Fernworthy originally consisted of three tenements, and according to Crossing, the farm, now demolished, belonged to a Farmer Lightfoot. Above the doorway was a stone bearing the inscription "L" and the date 1690. By 1702 the three tenements had become the property of John Clement. It is likely that the farm was of Saxon origin as "worthy" is a Saxon word meaning farmstead. There were certainly prehistoric settlements in the area and many of the surviving hut circles have also been submerged.

Work started on Fernworthy Reservoir in 1936, built to provide a supply of water to Newton Abbot, Bovey Tracey and Torquay. The upper valley of the South Teign river was dammed and this dam was the last to be constructed from local granite.

The building of the reservoir did not go smoothly and many problems were encountered. The great thunderstorm of 1938 had disastrous results. The works become flooded with two million gallons of water and 13,500 cubic feet of sand and silt that had to be removed. The onset of World War Two also caused further delays and it was not completed until 22nd June, 1942. In all, the actual cost of the reservoir was £246,000 as opposed to the estimate of £180,000. It covers 76 acres of land, is 685 feet wide, and can hold 380 million gallons of water.

In times of drought, some of what lies beneath the surface is exposed. As well as the two bridges and hut circles, there is Fernworthy Well and many tin mining remains in the form of spoil heaps, once so prominent on the banks of the South Teign river.

Plate 24. *Throwleigh* Chapman & Son

Plate 25. *Berrydown, Gidleigh* Chapman & Son

24. Throwleigh

Throwleigh is a small village near Chagford. This photograph shows Throwleigh Barton Cross which was restored in 1897 to commemorate Queen Victoria's sixtieth year as sovereign. Part of the inscription reads "This cross is erected upon the ancient base by the Rector and a Parishioner in the 60th year of the reign of her gracious majesty Queen Victoria".

In Throwleigh churchyard is the shaft of a cross, recently found whilst renovating The Barton farmhouse. It is probable that this originally belonged to the Throwleigh Barton Cross.

The church is dedicated to St Mary the Virgin and is mainly fifteenth century although the priest's doorway is thought to be thirteenth century.

There are many old houses dating from two or three centuries ago.

Nearby is Wonson, a farm where the M.P. for Okehampton, William Northmore, lived during the eighteenth century. He was a gambler who is reputed to have lost £17,000 at a game of cards. It was the ace of diamonds that let him down and he painted a picture of this on his bedroom wall as a constant reminder of his loss.

Throwleigh, as with many other places in this area, has been inhabited by man for centuries. The nearby common has many examples of hut circles, which deserve closer inspection

25. Berrydown, Gidleigh

Berrydown, once a Dartmoor farm, stands on the outskirts of the village of Gidleigh near Chagford, and it originates from the fourteenth century, when it was built for Ralph de Berridon. He is known to have occupied the farm in 1332 and it later passed to his son, Simon. It then changed hands and became the property of John Rowe. The 1572 South Tawton Rolls state that a "John Rowe of Berydon" was living there. The local Endicott family married into the Rowe family at some stage, and it may have been Sir John Endicott who became related to the Rowes. He went to America in 1628, after suffering religious persecution here. It is known that a man who lived at Berrydown during this period went to America with the Pilgrims and, consequently, the King partly destroyed the house in retaliation, so it is possible that Endicott is the man concerned.

A descendent of the above John Rowe was a local builder and he re-built Berrydown in 1665 as a wedding present for his wife. It is thought to have remained in the Rowe and Endicott families until 1956.

Plate 26. *Lower Street, Chagford* Chapman & Son

Plate 27. *The Market Square, Chagford* Valentine & Son

32

26 & 27. Chagford

Chagford is a popular Dartmoor town which has managed to retain its charm. Lower Street pictured above has buildings dating back several centuries. One of these is the sixteenth century Bishop's House attached to another building which was originally all one dwelling. The Bishop's House has a two storey porch and the upper floor overhangs on two moulded corbels. The Bishop of Exeter used to stay here on his annual visits.

The former Moor Park Hotel in Lower Street is nineteenth century. It has now been converted to dwellings. This street leads to the square and the Market House. This is the site of an older building which was called "The Shambles". It was supposed to be called the Market House but its state of delapidation resulted in the more appropriate nickname. It also had an open drain a few yards in front of it. In 1862, The Shambles was demolished and in the July of that year, the north-east cornerstone of the new octagonal building, seen in the lower photograph, was laid by Constance Hames, wife of the Rector. The architect was Mr Herbert Williams and the contractors were Messrs W. Stone and T. Ball.

On fair days, the market square was used for the sale of animals and for market traders and stalls. The toll board can be seen in a local museum. The market house today is converted into shops.

Chagford was one of Devon's Stannary towns where miners brought their tin for weighing and coining. The square once had a Stannary Court building which is reputed to have suddenly collapsed in 1617.

Tinning and farming have been Chagford's main industries but the former industry no longer exists. Between 1800 and 1848, woollen factories owned by a Mr Berry were in operation. One is now the Moorland Hotel, in Mill Street.

The town did not have a railway station, unlike the neighbouring town of Moretonhampstead. Although one was proposed, it was never built and Chagford had to rely upon the stage coach and later, the omnibus link. The G.W.R. bus service depot used to be behind Rock House at the junction of Lower Street and Southcombe Street. It was the first service of its kind in Devon and began in 1904 with a steam bus, later replaced by a motor bus. The service ran between Chagford and Moretonhampstead.

Buried in St Michael's churchyard is James Perrott, the Dartmoor guide and originator of the Dartmoor letterboxes. Opposite the church is the building where Sidney Godolphin was supposed to have been killed during the Civil War.

Plate 28. *Fingle Bridge Tea Shelter* Chapman & Son

28. Fingle Bridge Tea Shelter

The accessibility of popular areas for excursions and picnics improved greatly with the advent of the railways, motor car and bicycle. One place whose picturesque scenery attracted many visitors was Fingle Bridge near Drewsteignton.

Spanning the River Teign, this packhorse bridge, which is thought to date from the sixteenth century, was largely used by traders in corn milling and the production of fuel, charcoal and bark from the surrounding woods. These products often found their way to Exeter, Okehampton and Crediton.

From 1897, Jessie Ashplant, a Drewsteignton woman, catered for the visitors by providing pots of tea near the bridge. This service must have been well received because in 1907, a proper tea shelter was erected which offered some protection if the weather was unfavourable. This new shelter had a corrugated roof to which the local landowner objected. So it had to be covered with bracken and furze to blend in with its surroundings. This can clearly be seen in the photograph.

In 1929, this tea shelter was replaced by a hardier structure, and in 1957 the present Angler's Rest was built. It is owned by a descendant of Jessie Ashplant and so has remained in the family for over ninety years.

The photograph shows Jessie Ashplant in the dark dress, her two daughters, Edith on the left and Mary Ann on the right, both holding trays, and Jessie's son George in the foreground. Sitting in the tea shelter are customers for afternoon tea.

Above the shelter can be seen the steep slope leading up to Prestonbury Castle, an Iron Age hill fort.

Plate 29. *Drewsteignton* Chapman & Son

29. Drewsteignton

This is a small village near Chagford and not far from Fingle Bridge. The village square is of Saxon origin with the houses built in the defensive pattern, and a well, now covered by the road, situated in the centre. This Saxon layout is not so apparent now as the western end of the village was badly damaged by fire over a century ago. The Domesday Survey shows that the manor was held by Drogo de Teign, and during the reigns of Henry II and Richard I, it was held by another Drogo de Teign.

There were claims by antiquarians, including Polwhele, that the village's name was derived from "Druids town on the River Teign", but today this theory is dismissed as fanciful.

The whole area surrounding Drewsteignton was inhabited by Neolithic and Iron Age man, evidence of which can be seen in the numerous hut circles, Spinsters' Rock and the Iron Age hill fort, Prestonbury Castle.

It is not known exactly when the church was built, but it is thought to have been erected on the site of a very early religious establishment. The font is Norman and the north aisle is probably fourteenth century. It is dedicated to the Holy Trinity.

In the fifteenth century, much of the surrounding land was owned by the Carew family. In 1791, they sold it off in lots and the main buyers were a farming family, the Ponsfords, who became Lords of the Manor.

The early sixteenth century Church Cottage, left of the lychgate, was left to the parish by Peter Edgcombe in 1546. It served as a place of refuge for male vagrants. In 1931, it was purchased by public subscription and presented to the church in memory of William Ponsford who was the last squire of the parish and churchwarden from 1901 - 1931. Female vagrants were housed in Ladyhouse which can be found outside the east gate of the church in an area known as Churchgate.

By the mid nineteenth century, Drewsteignton had become an important village due to improved roads between the farms and neighbouring villages. Trades included quarrying at the Drewsteignton Lime Rock Quarries and mining at a nearby copper mine which also produced silver and tin.

In 1875 a board school was established for about 140 children.

There were three public houses; The Golden Lion, The Old Inn and The New Inn. The latter later became the Druids Arms, but it changed again to the Drewe Arms at the request of Julian Drewe who was responsible for the building of Castle Drogo.

Plate 30. *Jay's Grave, near Manaton* Chapman & Son

Plate 31. *Foxworthy Mill, near Lustleigh* Unknown

30. Jay's Grave

On the Ashburton to Chagford road is a place where it is crossed by a track linking Manaton and Natsworthy. Here is the burial place of Kitty Jay, marked by a small mound at the side of the road. She was a parish apprentice at the turn of the eighteenth century, who lived in a small cottage on the Forder Estate, owned by Mr W. Nosworthy.

Kitty Jay is reputed to have worked at Canna Farm, at the foot of Easdon Hill. When she became pregnant, her lover abandoned her and, unable to cope with the shame, she hanged herself in a barn at Canna.

Suicides were denied a churchyard burial in those days and instead were laid to rest at crossroads, so that their spirits would be unable to find their way home again.

In 1852, a farm labourer, George Leamon, who was employed by Mr James Bryant from Hedge Barton, had cause to open the grave whilst digging over the ground and mixing it with lime for the purpose of obtaining a good manure for the farm. Human bones and a skull were discovered which were found to be those of an adult female. They were re-interred on the same site. Fresh flowers are laid daily on the grave, and the identity of the person responsible remains a mystery.

31. Foxworthy Mill

It is not known exactly how old Foxworthy Mill is but it has certainly been in existence since 1603, when it is documented in a grant of 17th July of that year, giving the right to cut timber for repairs to a gentleman named Foxford.

Another document in 1614 shows that Robert Foxford conveyed Foxworthy estate and the mill to Edward Furlonge, with his rights over Lustleigh Cleave.

The principal machinery at the mill was for threshing corn, and water diverted from the River Bovey into a leat turned the mill wheel. It was in use as late as 1878 and the last miller was Simon Martin who had a donkey called "Black Jack". The building began to fall into disrepair, but in 1885, Mr Hunt purchased it for £1750 and saved it from ruin. The mill wheel was replaced by one bearing the inscription, "C. H. Reed. Chagford. Millwright. 1892". Until recently, the mill wheel was used to generate 7 kw of electricity for use in the house.

In 1920, the mill was let to a farmer, Henry Leaman, who built a small dairy to the rear of the house.

The thatch has since disappeared and has been replaced by a corrugated asbestos roof. Some of the old grindstones have been incorporated into the garden path and the cottage floor in front of the hearth.

Plate 32. *Manor House, North Bovey* Chapman & Son

Plate 33. *Hall House, Lustleigh* Unknown

32. Manor House, North Bovey

Built in the style of a Tudor castle, this impressive Manor House was completed in 1907. In 1880, W. H. Smith, founder of the bookshop empire and later to become Viscount Hambledon, had purchased 5,000 acres of land and property in the North Bovey area. His son, the second Viscount Hambledon, commissioned the building of this property on a piece of the land.

The architect was Walter Mills and the master builder was Lewis Bearne. Together they designed and built this magnificent house surrounded by some of England's most splendid scenery.

The Hambledon family had links with North Bovey for nearly fifty years until Lord Hambledon's death in 1928. The whole estate was sold and the Manor House eventually became the property of the Great Western Railway Company, who turned it into a hotel, complete with golf course.

In 1935-6, extensions in keeping with the style of architecture were undertaken. In 1983, due to government policy, the hotel was sold to a private buyer. It remains a popular holiday hotel.

33. Hall House, Lustleigh

This delightful building is the former Hall House of the Manor of Wreyland and is situated about a quarter of a mile from the village of Lustleigh.

The name Wreyland means land by the Wrey, which is a stream that flows into the River Bovey. Hall House is on its east bank, and is one of about six houses.

The original building dates from the fourteenth century, but the present structure is largely sixteenth and seventeenth century and the porch is dated 1680. In his book *Small Talk at Wreyland*, Cecil Torr says, "I decided not to sacrifice the seventeenth century work in order to restore the fourteenth. ..... There was originally a hall, with a screen across it, and a gallery projecting out beyond the screen on corbels."

Hall House was once used for the sittings of the Manor Court, but this practice ceased on 14th February, 1871. It has been the home of several notable families such as the younger son of the first Earl of Devon, Thomas de Courtney; a knight of the Garter, John Dynham; the Earls of Bath and the Earls and Marquesses of Northampton. It was also inhabited more recently by the Torr family, to whom Cecil Torr was related. His book, which he started at Christmas 1916, was published for private circulation. In it he reminisces about his memories and those of his father and grandfather. It offers an insight into life in a small Devon village before the motor car had made its impact on village life.

Plate 34. *Bellever Tor and the Cherrybrook* Unknown

Plate 35. *Pound Street, Moretonhampstead* Chapman & Son

34. Bellever Tor and the Cherrybrook

Bellever Tor stands not far from Postbridge at a height of 1456 feet above sea level. The land it stands on used to belong to Bellever Farm, one of the ancient tenements. It was the site of one of the moor's great events, the annual picnic held by the Dart Vale Harriers and known as Bellaford Day. People came from miles around and would watch the horse and hound races around the tor. Sadly, this moorland festivity has not been held since the 1930s.

This photograph is taken from below the Higher Cherrybrook Bridge. The source of the Cherrybrook can be found north-east of Brown's House near Broad Down.

In 1930, the Bellever area was sold to the Forestry Commission and over the years has been relentlessly planted with the afforestation we see today. Gone forever is the view we see here.

35. Pound Street, Moretonhampstead

With its thatched houses built so close together, Pound Street was the victim of fires in the nineteenth century. On 11th September, 1839 at 1am, fire broke out in the The White Horse Inn, kept by Samuel Gray. Sparks were carried on the wind to the thatched roofs and both sides of Pound Street were soon ablaze. Three horse-drawn fire appliances had to be summoned from Exeter; The Little West, the Norwich Union and the Sun engines. Although nine or ten houses were more or less gutted, no lives were lost.

Another fire broke out on 10th August, 1854 at 2am, but it was not known how this one started. The worst affected areas were again Pound Street and also Court Street. Experience of former fires had taught the Mortonians that organisation was of prime importance, and men clambered onto the roofs to brush burning embers from the thatch. Human chains kept the two Moretonhampstead fire engines supplied with water from nearby brooks. Ten houses were badly damaged in Pound Street and many people were consequently homeless.

Today, much of the thatch has been replaced by tiled roofs.

Plate 36. *Warren House Inn, near Postbridge* Unknown

Plate 37. *Inside the Warren House Inn* Charles Worcester & Co.

36 & 37. The Warren House Inn

The original inn stood on the south side of the road and was called "New Inn". It served as the local alehouse for the miners of the nearby Birch, Golden Dagger and Vitifer Mines. A warren was established in the locality and this enabled the landlord to provide rabbit pie with the scrumpy and ale.

There is an old tale told about the "New Inn". One winter's night, bad weather forced a gentleman to seek accommodation here. In his room, curiosity got the better of him and he opened up a wooden chest. To his horror, it contained the body of a man. In the morning he confronted his hosts with his gruesome discovery. He was calmly informed that the wife's father had died a couple of weeks previously and that due to the incessant snow and ice, they had been unable to transport his body for burial at the church. So instead, it had been well salted to await a respite in the weather.

This inn was demolished in 1845 and a new one built on the opposite side of the road the same year. This was at first called "The Moreton Inn". A tablet in the wall says "I. Wills, Septr 18 1845". It stands at a height of 1425 feet above sea level and is the second highest inn in England, the highest being in Derbyshire. It was not unknown for miners to lodge here during the week as many came from several miles away to work at the mines.

Jonas Coaker, renowned for his poetry, was landlord for a while. Crossing tells of an amusing incident when a party of miners invaded the premises. They were extremely rowdy and intent upon mischief. Jonas felt obliged to seek the safety of the moor, while these men were left to consume the liquor at their leisure.

In 1894, Tommy Hext took over as landlord. He stood over six feet tall and had a long beard. Liquor was drawn from barrels into enamel jugs at the back of the inn and the ale was often served in quart size mugs.

The peat fire is reputed to have been burning for well over one hundred years and it has been claimed that burning embers from the original inn's fire were brought across the road on a shovel and placed in the new hearth.

The bungalow to the extreme right of the plate was built at the turn of the century as miners' accommodation. Its local name was "Cape Horn" and it no longer exists.

The "King's Oven Bungalow", on the north side of the road towards the centre of the photograph, was also built at the turn of the century for Moses Bawden who became the Manager of the Vitifer and Golden Dagger Mines. This too has sadly disappeared, demolished in 1976.

Plate 38. *Temperance Hotel, Postbridge* Chapman & Son

Plate 39. *Old and New Bridges, Ockery* Kingsway Seines

38. Temperance Hotel, Postbridge

This hostelry is now the East Dart Hotel but last century, as the sign indicates, it was known as "Webb's Temperance Hotel". John Webb, who had been the Captain of Hexworthy Mine, bought the hotel which he ran successfully. On his death, it passed to his son, also named John, who was married to a teetotal wife, Lizzie, who heartily disapproved of alcohol and, therefore, her husband's inheritance.

Constant nagging from his wife and a Sunday sermon preaching about the evils of drink finally proved too much, and John returned home from church and emptied all the bottles and kegs holding alcoholic beverages into a ditch outside. This intoxicating liquid flowed down the slight incline into the East Dart river with, one might assume, an interesting effect on the fish!

According to folklore, from that day onwards at 3am each morning, a bloodhound runs out from Moretonhampstead to Postbridge to lick up the last dregs. The only alcohol served on the premises from then on was home-brewed cider.

The left-hand side of the building has been altered slightly and is now the Huntsman's Bar, happily selling alcohol once more.

39. Old and New Bridges, Ockery

These two bridges span the Blackbrook River near Princetown. The larger bridge carries the B3212 road while the clapper bridge forms part of the old packhorse track. To the left of the photograph can be seen the dwelling known as The Ockery. This was built in 1809 by Thomas Tyrwhitt for the French officer-prisoners of war, and two such officers, Boyer and Rochambeau, lived here. Originally, the house was single storey with an exterior gallery and verandah.

During the late nineteenth century, an elderly lady, Mrs Kistel, lived here. Her son enlarged the house making it two storeys high and in the process, removed the gallery and verandah. The Kistel family occupied the house until 1914. Soon afterwards it was demolished.

On the right can be seen the barn which was used by the Kistel family.

Plate 40. *Princetown and the Duchy Hotel* Chapman & Son

Plate 41. *Prison officers at Princetown* F. Frith & Co.

40. Princetown & the Duchy Hotel

One of the hosts of The Duchy Hotel, to the left of the photograph, was Aaron Rowe whose daughter Beatrice married George Stevens, illustrator of William Crossing's *Guide to Dartmoor*. His grandfather, James Rowe, had witnessed the rise and progress of Princetown and he appears to have been a man of many trades. In 1815 he was a master blacksmith. He became landlord of the Railway Inn and was also a competent dentist. He passed on the tools of this latter trade to his son James Julian Rowe, father of Aaron.

Sometime after 1850, James Rowe Junior took over The Duchy Hotel. It was in need of considerable restoration with its moss covered walls and nettles growing up through the ground floor.

Once restored, it became a thriving hostelry which was eventually passed on to Aaron. It boasted many important guests including George V and Queen Mary when they were the Prince and Princess of Wales, Edward VIII when he was Prince of Wales, Conan Doyle, Baring-Gould and Arnold Bennett.

The flooring in the entrance bears the words "Welcome the Coming" facing the arrivals, and "Speed the Departing" facing those departing.

41. Dartmoor Prison Officers

Dartmoor Prison was the brainchild of Thomas Tyrwhitt, Private Secretary to the Prince of Wales who was later to become King George IV.

During the Napoleonic Wars many French prisoners were held under appalling conditions in rotting hulks off the port of Plymouth. This gave rise to the fear of both epidemics and rioting from the incarcerated prisoners. Tyrwhitt, who was also Lord Warden of the Stannaries, recommended Princetown as an ideal site for the construction of a prison to accommodate these men. The foundation stone was laid on 20th March, 1806, by Tyrwhitt himself, and there were seven buildings in all in an area of 30 acres.

The first Governor, Captain Isaac Cotgrave, was appointed in 1808 and shortly afterwards, the first prisoners arrived. The number rose to nine thousand.

In 1812 Britain was plunged into war with America which resulted in the arrival of a large number of American prisoners.

1814 saw the declaration of peace between England and America, and in 1815 the same was declared with France. On 10th February, 1816, the last of the prisoners departed.

The buildings became a convict prison in 1850 and, on 2nd November, 95 prisoners arrived.

This photograph was taken about 1910. Note the clay pipes and metal jugs.

Plate 42. *Two Bridges Hotel* Unknown

Plate 43. *Two Bridges Hotel* Unknown

42 & 43. Two Bridges Hotel

The introduction of turnpike roads saw the establishment of many wayside inns, built to cater for the weary traveller. The Saracen's Head at Two Bridges, later to be named The Two Bridges Hotel, was one such inn.

It was Sir Francis Buller of Prince Hall who inaugurated the construction of the inn at the west end of one of his newtakes and named it The Saracen's Head after his family's crest. Its appearance then is not as we know it now. Originally it was very small but was substantially added to during the beginning of this century. The old tavern is still identifiable as the central section where one of the entrances is situated.

In November, 1813, a notice appeared in a local paper: "John Pooke begs to announce that he has taken and entered the above inn". He had formerly been a carrier from Exeter to Moretonhampstead and Plymouth but had ceased this trade upon taking over The Saracen's Head. A gentleman by the name of Peter Chaffe was the host.

It is known that in 1840, the landlord was John Hamlyn, and during the 1880s, Kelly's Directory shows a Mrs Mary Smith as landlady. She managed the inn with her two sons.

Henry Trinaman took over the running of the inn in 1893 and he changed the name to The Saracen's Head Hotel. He became known locally as "Trinny" and appears to have been very popular. He was responsible for the enlarging of the building and eventually changing the name again to The Two Bridges Hotel.

It became a notable centre for fishing and bloodsports, with the hunting of rabbits, foxes, polecats and golden eagles, the latter of which were believed to be lamb-killers.

Eden Phillpotts featured the hotel in his novel *The River* where it was called the Ring o' Bells. His characters were based upon actual people living in the vicinity, for example, Mark Trout was based upon the Hotel's ostler, George French who lived with his family at Beardown Lodge.

The smaller of the two bridges carries the old turnpike road and was built in 1792. The newer bridge was not constructed until 1931 and it was given the name "Prince Edward Bridge". Therefore as the name Two Bridges existed before 1792, it has been derived from some other source. If two bridges existed over the rivers Dart and Cowsic, one can only surmise where where they might once have stood and Hemery feels it is unlikely that Beardown clapper is one of these.

Of course, it could have evolved from the word "torbrygge" meaning "at the bridge" which was a word found to be documented for the area in the reign of Henry VI and could refer to a former clapper between Crockern Farm and Cowsic Foot, reputed to have been a casualty of a spate during the early nineteenth century.

Plate 44. *River Dart in flood at Dartmeet, 1938* Chapman & Son

Plate 45. *River Dart in flood at Dartmeet, 1938* Chapman & Son

44 & 45. Dartmeet 1938

These two photographs illustrate Dartmeet after a dramatic thunderstorm on August Bank Holiday, which affected much of Devon.

The tremendous electrical storm started at 1am on Thursday, 4th August, but the full force of it did not arrive until three hours later. A newspaper report stated that "thunder rolled like batteries of guns, torrential rain and hail came down continually, and lightning was discharged with vicious cracks". The massive volume of water that had fallen on high Dartmoor resulted in the rivers bursting their banks, as seen here. Although the clapper bridge at Dartmeet was not damaged on this occasion, others such as the one at Buckland Bridge were swept clean away. Mr E. F. Windeatt, on behalf of the Teign Naturalist Association, expressed the hope that this bridge would be restored as it was a place "famous almost throughout the world".

In Ashburton, North Street and St Lawrence Lane took on the appearance of rivers rather than roads. Houses backing onto the River Yeo suffered flooding to a depth of three feet, and in The Globe Hotel the water reached to the top of the counters in the bars. In all, 5.57 inches of rain fell here.

The damage left behind by the storm was extensive. Twenty-one sheep and two cows were killed by lightning at Dartington Hall Estate, near Totnes. A Dartmoor farmer lost five bullocks after they were struck by a single flash of lightning and there were many other similar losses of livestock suffered.

Torquay had an estimated £50,000 worth of damage and a substantial loss of trade for local businesses due to flooding. The River Wrey at Bovey Tracey overflowed, flooding shops and houses and bringing traffic to a standstill.

Damage on a large scale was also recorded at Moretonhampstead, Okehampton, Tavistock, Exeter, Exmouth and Minehead.

The resulting flood waters at Dartmeet brought out observers. One photograph shows two figures standing by the bridge and another standing by the sign. The photographer from Chapman & Son obviously considered it was a spectacle worth recording, too.

Plate 46. *Widecombe-in-the-Moor* Unknown

Plate 47. *Uncle Tom Cobleigh and all.* E. Scott

46 & 47. Widecombe-in-the-Moor

Situated in the heart of Dartmoor, Widecombe is one of Devon's most frequented villages. The shop featured in the top photograph was owned by Mr R. Kernick and called "The Smithy Shop". It catered mainly for the visitor, stocking a large assortment of wares including postcards, pottery, toby jugs and general souvenirs. On the roof is a picture of Uncle Tom Cobleigh an' All. The building is now replaced by a modern shop.

To the left of the photograph is the old smithy which ceased working in the 1950s due to the increasingly popular motor car. It was, until recently, a small museum. The elm and yew trees standing in the two granite surrounds, have been felled, the former a victim of Dutch Elm Disease no doubt.

The bottom photograph shows Edward Dunn playing the part of Uncle Tom Cobleigh. He trained his grey mare to play the part while he himself took great delight in dressing up in his white smock and top hat. He also appeared in the film "Escape", adapted from John Galsworthy's novel, and sold thousands of autographed postcards of himself.

Edward Dunn died at the age of 67 in 1938, after playing Uncle Tom Cobleigh for many years. He claimed to be a direct descendent of the character as the Cobleighs and Dunns had intermarried. His great-uncle was the first man to sing the ballad of Widecombe Fair to Rev. Sabine Baring-Gould who collected Westcountry songs. This song was later sung at the fairs by Edward Dunn on the village green. He discovered a new verse in the family bible showing that Tom Pearse was recompensed for the death of his mare, and sang it in September 1914:

"And they all walked home from Widecombe Fair,
All along, down along, out along lee,
Though they buried the other they bought Tom Pearse another,
Did Bill Brewer, Jan Stewer, Peter Gurney, Peter Davy
        Dan'l Whiddon, Harry Hawk,
Old Uncle Tom Cobleigh an' all,
Old Uncle Tom Cobleigh an' all".

55

Plate 48. *Beatrice Chase* Chapman & Son

48. Beatrice Chase

Beatrice Chase was born at Harrow in Middlesex in 1874. Although not a native of Dartmoor, she keenly adopted the area when she moved to Widecombe-in-the-Moor early this century. Her real name was Olive Katherine Parr, and she was proud of her claim to royal descent. One of her ancestors was brother to Henry VIII's sixth wife, Catherine Parr.

When she moved to her house Venton with her mother, she began to write romantic books about life on Dartmoor. She wrote under the pseudonym of Beatrice Chase, and this is the name that most people recognise. Her books, although romantic and sentimental, depict a way of life that is no longer with us today. Old farming practices and a time untouched by widespread commercialism were recorded and subsequently preserved in print.

Initially, the books she wrote were distributed by her publisher, but later in life she began to sell them, together with postcards, from a window at her own home. She is pictured here outside the same window. The little sign above her head reads, "Books and Postcards". Two of her best known books are *The Heart of the Moor* and *Through a Dartmoor Window*.

In 1930, Beatrice Chase became a professional photographer and later signed a contract with Raphael Tuck to produce Dartmoor postcards. In 1931, her own book, *Dartmoor Snapshots* was published. Again, these are of social, historical interest as they visually portray a former way of country life.

During her younger days, Beatrice Chase suffered an emotional blow when her fiancé was killed. Her strong faith helped her through this crisis, and it was this faith which prompted her to build a small chapel at Venton. She began a "White Knights' Crusade" which promoted moral living. In a book kept near her chapel altar, she entered the names of all soldiers who agreed to lead honourable and clean lives. This crusade had quite a following for a while.

Towards the latter part of her life, Beatrice Chase began to dislike the continual calling of sightseers and her reputation suffered accordingly. She became a recluse, shutting herself away at Venton. Her days ended in hospital two days before her 81st birthday. She is buried in Widecombe churchyard, near to her mother.

Friend and author, John Oxenham, called her "My Lady of the Moor" in his novel of the same name. It is a title that has stayed with her.

Plate 49. *Venton Cottage* Chapman & Son

Plate 50. *Interior of Venton Chapel* Chapman & Son

49. Venton Cottage

At Venton is a most attractive thatched farmhouse situated on the outskirts of Widecombe and was for many years the home of Beatrice Chase. The end wing where she lived was known as Venton Cottage.

Beatrice Chase and her mother came to live here at the turn of the century, and a few years later an extra wing was added to the cottage. It was Miss Chase's mother, affectionately known as the "Rainbow Maker", who drew up the plans for the extension. There were "no architect, no contract and consequently no contractor". It was also the "Rainbow Maker's" decision to have the famous window set into a curved wall, which did not meet the approval of the workmen. However, on completion, they had to admit that it looked acceptable. In all, nine men were employed to extend the house, comprising carpenters, masons and a thatcher. As with the original part of the house, granite from the moor and water from the River Dart were used in its construction, making it a truly indigenous house.

50. Venton Chapel

Both Beatrice Chase and her mother were devout Roman Catholics, and in 1908 they had a small thatched barn adjacent to the house converted into a chapel. They prayed here daily and a priest from Ashburton would on occasions make the journey to Venton to take Latin Mass.

The interior of the chapel was always clean and well looked after. The walls were painted white, offsetting the black rafters and red-wood seats, and a lamp burned continuously outside the entrance. Inside the chapel could be found her "Book of White Knights" at the foot of the altar, a missal, books of devotion, prayer books and a visitors' book bound in olive wood.

The chapel was always kept open for passers-by, but Beatrice Chase became increasingly dismayed at peoples' disrespect. When she had the chapel enlarged, an inner glass door leading to it was kept locked. A chosen few, mainly women, were told where to find the keys. Remarking upon this, Beatrice Chase said, "In this way, I have enabled well-bred women to use the chapel even more freely than before, but, on the other hand, I have excluded the other sort."

Today the lamps burn no more and the chapel has fallen into disuse.

Plate 51. *Holne Park, Ashburton* Chapman & Son

Plate 52. *Lower Lodge, Buckland* Chapman & Son

51. Holne Park

After the Norman Conquest, the area on the Holne side of the River Dart came into the possession of Sheriff Baldwin de Rivers and William de Falaise, two Norman noblemen. For the next 800 years it remained in the possession of their families until 1885, when the Hon. Richard Maitland Westenra Dawson, third son of the First Earl of Daltrey, purchased the estate. He and his family resided at Holne Park, extending the building to become a stately mansion.

There were three Dawson children, Dick, Norah and Molly. Dick, serving with the 3rd Battalion of the Coldstream Guards during World War One, was killed in action while commanding No 2 Company. A window in Holne church is dedicated to him. Molly had previously died of consumption, and Norah was to die of cancer ten years after the death of Mrs Dawson who passed away on 28th February, 1932. She had survived her husband by eighteen years.

In 1926, Mrs Dawson had decided to auction some of the farms on the estate. The auction was held at the Seymour Hotel in Totnes on the 17th September, where 1237 acres came under the hammer. Much of it went to sitting tenants. Some of the farms sold included Michelcombe, Wellpritton and Shuttaford.

After Mrs Dawson's death the remainder of the estate was sold as, due to a dispute with her mother, Norah did not inherit.

52. Lower Lodge, Buckland

This is the Lower Lodge at Buckland, situated not far from Buckland Bridge which spans the River Webburn just before it joins the River Dart. Built in the seventeenth century, it was originally two cottages but has now been converted to one dwelling and is also a listed building. It has attracted many artists over the years, and a sketch by Turner is housed in the Tate Gallery. The two figures standing by the door are thought to be Mr and Mrs Warren who lived here during the early years of this century.

The Manor of Buckland was owned by the Bastard family and their seat was at Buckland Court. During the early nineteenth century, they purchased the adjoining Manor of Ausewell which was about 700 acres. Much of this land was planted with trees, firs and shrubs creating the famous Buckland Drives. There were three drives in all, two on the wooded hillside and a third by the river. Lower Lodge was situated by one of these drives.

In 1860, this advertisement appeared in the *Totnes Times*, "Drives through B.J.P. Bastard's property at Buckland-in-the Moor will be open during Summer (exc. Sundays). Please enter by Higher Ausewell Drive and leave by Holne Bridge Lodge."

In 1920, the estate was sold, and in the photograph a sale notice can be seen to the left of the front door. During the 1950s, the estate was broken up and sold off in separate lots.

Plate 53. *Buckfast Abbey before restoration* W. R. Gay

Plate 54. *Rebuilding of Buckfast Abbey* Unknown

53 & 54. Buckfast Abbey

Buckfast Abbey has a long history and it is commonly thought that King Cnut ordered the construction of the Abbey in 1018, possibly in reparation for the Danes' desecration of Tavistock Abbey in 997, and that the first monks came from Tavistock and Winchester Abbeys. However, it is highly likely that the site was used for religious purposes prior to this and Baring-Gould aired the opinion that its history goes back to the sixth century when Celtic saints including St Petrock and St Brannock travelled throughout Devon and Cornwall. Many of the early churches of this time were dedicated to St Petrock and later had dependencies on the Abbey, suggesting some earlier connection. But the origins of the Abbey must, for now, remain in obscurity until such a time when undisputable documentary evidence comes to light.

Originally, Benedictine monks resided here but later, Cistercian monks were installed. They were great traders and specialised in the wool trade and were admitted to the Guild of Merchants of Totnes in 1236.

The Dissolution in 1539 took its toll of the Abbey and on 25th February of that year, the deed of surrender was signed by the Abbot, Gabriel Donne; the Prior, Arnold Gye and nine other monks in front of William Petre, the King's Commissioner. The Abbey roof was stripped of lead and the five bells were bought for the Buckfastleigh church. The monastic buildings were left to fall into a ruinous state, as with many others throughout the country.

In 1806, John Berry erected a house in the grounds, and in 1882, French Benedictine monks purchased it. A German monk, Dom Boniface Natter was appointed as Abbot in 1903, the first for nearly 365 years. He died tragically at sea three years later and was replaced by Dom Anscar Vonier, also a German. It was Abbot Vonier who resolved to rebuild the Abbey in memory of his predecessor, relying upon funds received from kind benefactors, and the first stone was laid on 5th January, 1907. Brother Peter was the sole stone mason and he had to train other brothers in the craft. However, only five or six monks could be spared at any one time to help re-build the Abbey and the average number was four, usually Brother Hilarion, Brother Peter, Father Richard and Brother Ignatius.

It was not until 1932 that the newly re-erected Abbey was consecrated in a memorable ceremony, and its completion marked the end of a tremendous feat undertaken by so few.

The top photograph shows some of the remains of the old Abbey in the foreground before re-building commenced. The bottom photograph shows the Abbey under reconstruction.

Plate 55. *Church Steps, Buckfastleigh* Chapman & Son

64

55. Buckfastleigh & the Church Steps

These steps, 196 in all, are situated off Station Road and lead up to Holy Trinity Church. It is situated some distance from the town and according to legend, the church was supposed to have been built nearer the town but the devil kept removing the stones to the hilltop site. However, it has been suggested that the original population of the town lived in this higher area until the woollen industry removed them to the lower riverside area where the River Mardle provided the necessary power.

The church itself was built in the thirteenth century, although its distinctive spire is of a later date, and the list of vicars dates back to 1263. Ruins of an old Chantry Chapel can be found to the east of the church.

The tomb of Richard Cabell is west of the main entrance. He was a hell-raising individual, much feared throughout the neighbourhood. In 1656, he built Brook Manor near Buckfastleigh. He died in 1677, and his tomb was designed to be very strong so as to keep his evil spirit confined. But his spirit is reputed to escape on occasions and travel across the moor on horseback, followed by a pack of hell hounds. Arthur Conan Doyle is thought to have based his novel *The Hound of the Baskervilles* on this legend.

There was a settlement at Buckfastleigh as far back as the Saxon era and it later became a woollen manufacturing town. Today many associated buildings can still be seen, for example, the early to mid-nineteenth century mill buildings in Chapel Street. There were as many as six working mills here in the sixteenth century and it was an industry that continued until early this century, despite a slump in the wool trade during the last century, which badly affected the neighbouring town of Ashburton.

An influential family living in the town last century were the Hamlyns. In 1806, Joseph Hamlyn purchased a tannery and together with his three sons worked a fellmongering business. In 1846, the Hamlyns formed a limited company. By the turn of the century, the family owned the largest mill in the town. The Co-operative Wholesale Society bought it in 1920.

Not only did the Hamlyns provide employment in their mill, but they also provided the Town Hall and library, and in 1921, the town's playing fields.

Plate 56. *South Brent, Station Road and Square* Unknown

Plate 57. *Moorlands Hotel, Haytor* Unknown

66

56. South Brent

This village is dominated by Brent Hill from which it takes its name. From the top of the hill, which stands at 1017 feet, are extensive views over the South Hams and the south-eastern borders of Dartmoor.

The manors of Brent and Aish belonged to the Abbots of Buckfastleigh until the Dissolution when Henry VIII gave them to Sir William Petre. They remained in his family's ownership until the early 1800s.

St. Petrock's Church was built on an ancient religious site dating back to the seventh century when St. Petrock visited the area. Evidence of a Saxon church can be found in the belfry where several arches of the original structure remain. The tower dates from the Norman period and the font is also twelfth century.

In 1347, a Royal Charter granted permission for markets to be held. From a window in the Toll House, there used to hang a stuffed glove signifying freedom from arrest on market days.

South Brent has been an area of great industrial activity in the past. It was an important centre with its many tucking, corn and paper mills. In 1846, a peat and charcoal works was established at the nearby Shipley Bridge, and in 1848, the railway opened encouraging trade links as well as social trips. This line closed in 1964.

For a while, South Brent was the home of William Crossing. At the age of twenty, he entered his father's sail cloth factory, "Crossing, Phelp & Co." which produced canvas for the Devon ship building industry. Crossing junior neglected his duties in the factory which contributed to the financial difficulties of the company and it eventually closed. After his marriage to Emma Witheridge, he lived at Splatton in South Brent, from where he wrote many of his notable works including *Amid Devonia's Alps*.

57. Moorlands Hotel, Haytor

This popular hotel was built around the turn of the century near one of Dartmoor's best loved scenic attractions, Hey Tor. In 1958, another wing was added to the building to accommodate the rising number of tourists. Agatha Christie, the well known author, was a frequent visitor to the hotel.

However, in 1970, disaster struck. The Bovey Tracey police and about 250 guests were attending their annual ball, on 6th March of that year. Shortly after midnight, they found themselves being evacuated due to a fire which had broken out. Despite the blaze being fought by sixty firemen from ten fire engines, most of the upper storey was destroyed with substantial damage caused to the ground floor. The cause of the fire was thought to be faulty wiring, and the once prestigious three star hotel remained derelict for some years.

Fortunately, in 1984 it was re-opened, having been bought for the sum of £180,000 and then renovated to its former glory.

Plate 58. *Ilsington* Chapman & Son

Plate 59. *Ilsington* Unknown

58 & 59. Ilsington

Ilsington is a large parish on the south-eastern edge of Dartmoor which incorporates several hamlets including Liverton and Haytor Vale. The name is derived from Ilestintona, recorded in the Domesday Survey.

The church is dedicated to St Michael and is fourteenth century with fifteenth century alterations. The alterations were financially possible due to the industrial boom in the wool and tin trades during that period. John Ford, the Elizabethan dramatist, was baptised here on 12th April, 1586.

The church was sought as a place of refuge by Royalist soldiers after their defeat at the Battle of Bovey Tracey in 1646. However, they were eventually compelled to leave by their Cromwellian enemies.

Remains of a partially completed Manor House are situated to the east of the church, built by Sir Henry Ford, twice Secretary of State in Ireland during the reign of King Charles II. A school was later erected on part of the site.

The lychgate had an upper storey which housed a small school during the seventeenth century and it was constructed of shingle stone and wooden rafters. On 17th September, 1639, whilst the school was occupied by Mr H. Corbin, the schoolmaster, and seventeen pupils the building collapsed. A woman had passed through the Lychgate, letting it bang shut with disastrous results. Miraculously, no one was badly injured, and due to the wet weather, attendance had been lower than the usual 30 pupils. This incident occurred less than a year after another similar accident at Widecombe on 21st October, 1638.

Many locals used to be known as "Ilsington Greybacks". In 1727 William Candy left an area of land to trustees. Rents collected from this land were to be used to buy garments for those men who had served their farming apprenticeship in the parish. The cloth used to make the clothes was called "Parson's Grey" and the name given to these men was derived from this.

69

Plate 60. *Pinchaford, near Ilsington* Chapman & Son

60. Pinchaford

Pinchaford is in the parish of Ilsington, near Haytor Vale. This photograph shows the old bridge at Pinchaford which spanned the River Lemon. The replacement bridge, erected later, was washed away by a flood in the great storm of 4th August, 1938. A road bridge now stands near this spot.

The gentleman is William Cumming, who was born in 1839. During the early years of the century, he farmed at Pinchaford as a tenant. Here, he is seen leaning on his eval or dung-fork.

The source of the River Lemon is not far from Pinchaford. It rises near the disused Haytor Quarries and flows southwards through Dartmoor hamlets and woods.

The river used to serve as the main water supply for Ilsington as well as feeding local mills including that of Bagtor.

This area has fortunately remained a most attractive spot.

Bibliography

Baring-Gould, S. *A Book of Dartmoor* Methuen & Co. 1900
Belstone, A Guide to the Church of St Mary the Virgin (undated)
Billings, M. *Directory & Gazetteer of the County of Devon.* Billings, Birmingham 1857
Bray, E. *A Description of the Part of Devonshire bordering on the Tamar & the Tavy* John Murray, London 1836
Brown, T. *Tales of a Dartmoor Village* J. Stevens Cox 1973
Buckfastleigh, Guide to Holy Trinity Church, (undated)
Burnard, R. *Dartmoor Pictorial Records* Devon Books 1986
Chase, B. *Through a Dartmoor Window* Longmans, Green & Co. 1934
Chard, J. *Along the Lemon* Bossiney Books 1978
Chard, J. *Along the Teign* Bossiney Books 1981
Crossing, W. *Gems in a Granite Setting* Devon Books 1986
Crossing, W. *Guide to Dartmoor* David & Charles 1965
Crossing, W. *Stones of Dartmoor & their Story* Quay Publications (Brixham) 1987
Crossing, W. *The Teign From Moor to Sea* Quay Publications (Brixham) 1986
Dartmoor Preservation Association. *Misuse of a National Park* D.P.A. 1963
Day, K. F. *Eden Phillpotts on Dartmoor* David & Charles 1981
Drewsteignton, Guide to the Holy Trinity Church Drewsteignton Parochial Church Council 1986
Dymond, R. *Things New and Old Concerning the Parish of Widecombe-in-the-Moor* Torquay 1876.
Gentry, F. D. *Take Care of Your Fire and Candlelight* Devon Books 1985
Gill, C. *The Best History of Yelverton* The Grey House Press 1984.
Gill, C. (Ed) *Dartmoor: A New Study* David & Charles 1970
Green, C. *My Lady of the Moor* C. Green 1974
Greeves, T. *Tin Mines and Miners of Dartmoor* Devon Books 1986
Harris, H. *Industrial Archaeology of Dartmoor* David & Charles 1986
Hayter-Hames, J. *A History of Chagford* Phillimore & Co. Ltd. 1981
Hemery, E. *High Dartmoor* Robert Hale Ltd. 1983
Hemery, E. *Walking Dartmoor's Ancient Tracks* Robert Hale Ltd 1986
Holne Estate Auction Catalogue, 1926
Holne, A History of St Nicholas Books 1977
Hoskins, W. G. *Devon* Collins, London 1954
Hunt, C. *My Saxon Farm. The Story of Foxworthy* (unpublished)
St. Leger-Gordon, D. *Under Dartmoor Hills* Robert Hale Ltd 1954
Martin, E. W. *Dartmoor* Robert Hale Ltd 1958
Morris, J. (Ed) *Domesday Book: Devonshire* Phillimore & Co Ltd 1985
Price, J. *Visitor's Guide to Fingle Bridge* (undated)
Sanderson, R. *The Prison on the Moor* Westway Publication (undated)
Stanbrook, E. *Dartmoor During the Saxon Age* Dartmoor Magazine No 2 1986
Stéphan, Dom John *Buckfast Abbey* The Burleigh Press 1970
Thomas, R. *St. Peter's Church, Meavy, Devon* 1973
Torr, C. *Small Talk at Wreyland* Oxford University Press 1979
Totnes Times 1860 - 1938
Transactions of the Devonshire Association The Devonshire Association
Various, *Devon Town Trails* European Architectural Heritage Year 1975
Warden-Page, J. L. *The Rivers of Devon* Seeley & Co Ltd 1893
Western Morning News 1898-1987
White, W. *History, Gazetteer, and Directory of Devonshire* Robert Leader 1850
Woodcock, G. *Tavistock's Yesterdays Volume 1* G. Woodcock 1985
Wootton, M. & S. *The Little Book of Lydford - Facts and Legends* 1972
Wootton, M. & S. *Reminiscences of Tavistock* 1975
Worth, R. H. *Dartmoor* David & Charles 1967